PUZZLE SCHOOL

Susannah Leigh

Illustrated by Brenda Haw

Contents

Series Editor: Gaby Waters
Editor: Michelle Bates

121602<u>89</u>

About this book

This book is about Puzzle School and the children who go there. There are puzzles to solve on every double page. If you get stuck you can look at the answers on pages 31 and 32.

This is Greg. He is a pupil at Puzzle School.

This is Mrs. Smith. She is Greg's teacher at Puzzle School.

Puzzle School

On Monday, Mrs. Smith had some news for her class. "It's the school outing tomorrow," she said. "But I'm afraid I won't be here. There will be a new teacher coming for the day. She's called Miss Dibble." Then Mrs. Smith gave everyone a letter for their parents.

See you soon, Mrs. Smith!

Be good!

Puzzle School

Monday

Dear Parents

Tomorrow each class is going on an outing. I will not be here, but Miss Dibble will be in charge for the day. Come to Puzzle School as usual.
Please could all pupils bring a packed lunch.

From
Mrs. Smith
(Class teacher)

Things to spot

Miss Dibble, the new teacher, is a scatterbrain. She's always losing things. She has lost one of these things on every double page, starting on pages 6 and 7.

MISS DIBBLE

cup of tea

paint box

tissues

whistle

key

glasses

pencil

glue

recorder

chalk

scissors

book

SCARY THINGS

STICK-IT

Brian and Beryl
Brian and Beryl are in Greg's class. They are very naughty. See if you can spot the mischief they get into on every double page, from when Greg arrives at Puzzle School on pages 6-7.

Puzzle School pencils
Can you find the yellow puzzle school pencils? At least one has been left lying around on every double page, starting on page 6.

There aren't any yellow pencils on pages 28 and 29.

3

Getting ready

On Tuesday morning, Greg woke up bright and early, ready for school. He was very excited because today was the day of the school outing. He gobbled down his breakfast and began to get ready for school, but where were all his things? He needed his purple lunch box, his ink pen, his watch, a tennis ball – and his school bag to put everything in.

Can you find the things that Greg needs for school?

Hurry up, Greg, you'll be late.

Milk
Eggs
Bread

4

5

Walking to school

Greg walked to Puzzle School from his house each day. There was always lots to see and do on the way. Today the roads were not very busy but lots of the paths were blocked.

"Don't walk in the road, Greg," his mother called. "And remember, always cross at the striped crossings."

Can you see Puzzle School? (There is a picture of it on page 2.) What route should Greg take to get there?

Bye Ma!

In the playground

Greg arrived safely at Puzzle School. He ran into the playground and looked around for his best friend, Jack. Greg couldn't see him anywhere, but he saw his other friends. Amber was playing hopscotch. Katy was skipping with a red skipping rope. Ben was playing marbles. Ned was kicking a ball. Then at last he saw Jack. He was wearing his yellow baseball cap as usual.

Can you find all of Greg's friends?

Hello everyone!

Classroom in a muddle

All the children piled into their classrooms. Greg hung his bag on his peg. He looked at the room. Something was wrong. It was different from yesterday. Then Greg remembered that the painters had been in last night.

"Miss Dibble," he said to the new teacher, "Everything's been moved. Even our desks are in the wrong places."

Yesterday…

"Oh dear," said Miss Dibble, looking puzzled. "I'm afraid I don't know what this room looked like before. Can any of you remember?"

What has changed in the classroom? Can you find Greg's desk? (It matches his peg.)

Today...

Jobs to do

Soon everything was straightened out and Miss Dibble took the register.

"Now," she said when she had called out all their names. "Can somebody tell me what you usually do next?"

"The monitors have their jobs to do," Greg said helpfully, pointing to the chart on the wall. "There are plants to water and the rabbit to feed. There are pencils to sharpen and writing books to hand out. Someone has to wipe the blackboard, too."

But there was a problem. Things were missing. Where was the rabbit's carrot? What about the blackboard cleaner? There was no sign of the pencil pot or the yellow writing books, either. And what had happened to the watering can?

Who is doing what job today? Can you find the things they need?

Today is Tuesday
My name is Miss D

13

Miss Dibble is confused

Jack, Katy, Amber, Greg and Ned finished their jobs at last.

"Is it nearly time to go on the outing?" asked Greg.

"Soon," said Miss Dibble. "But first we have some work to do."

Katy wrote in her book.

Ben painted a picture.

They all sang songs.

Amber showed everyone a photograph of her new baby brother.

Jack did a drawing of the rabbit.

Suddenly, Miss Dibble looked at the clock. "It's nearly half past ten," she said. "Time to clear up. We can't go out until we do. Quick, hurry!"

But Miss Dibble's instructions were all muddled.

"Where should everything really go?" Jack whispered. Greg knew.

Do you?

In the hall

At last everything was tidy. Miss Dibble and her class went to the hall with the rest of the school.

"Where are we going on our outing?" Greg asked Miss Dibble on the way.

"Wait and see," she said as they joined the other classes in the hall. Greg wondered if she'd forgotten.

"Listen carefully," said Mrs. Meady, the head of the school. "One class is going swimming, one class is going ice skating and another class is going to the Dinosaur Park. Mr. Brain's class is visiting the Choco Factory and class four is going to Muddy Farm." She smiled. "The buses are waiting for you outside. But first of all, Mr. Brain's class are going to play their recorders for us."

While Mr. Brain's class was playing their recorders, Greg tried to figure out where his class was going. He saw that some of the children in the other classes had special equipment with them. That made it easier for him to guess.

Where are Greg's class going for their outing?

Bus trouble

Greg and his class were off to the Dinosaur Park! That sounded exciting.

The buses were waiting. Greg and his friends followed Miss Dibble outside the school. Then they climbed on board their bus.

Greg was curious...

What exactly is a dinosaur park?

Wait and see.

The buses roared off one by one.

Stan the driver turned the key...

...but a red warning light flashed on.

"Oh dear," said Stan. "What's wrong?"

Katy jumped down from the bus. "I might be able to help," she said. "My dad's a mechanic." Katy looked at the engine. "I can see the problem," she said.

What has Katy spotted?

Map reading

Stan found some oil in the school garage and filled the engine.
At last they were on their way!

"We're off to the Dinosaur Park," everyone sang, as the bus
wound its way down the street. Left out of the school gates, then left
again, second right, left again and they were at a crossroads.

"Which way now?" called Stan.
"I can't read the map and drive at the
same time."

"We'll help!"called Greg and Jack.

**Where are they on the map?
Which way should they go?**

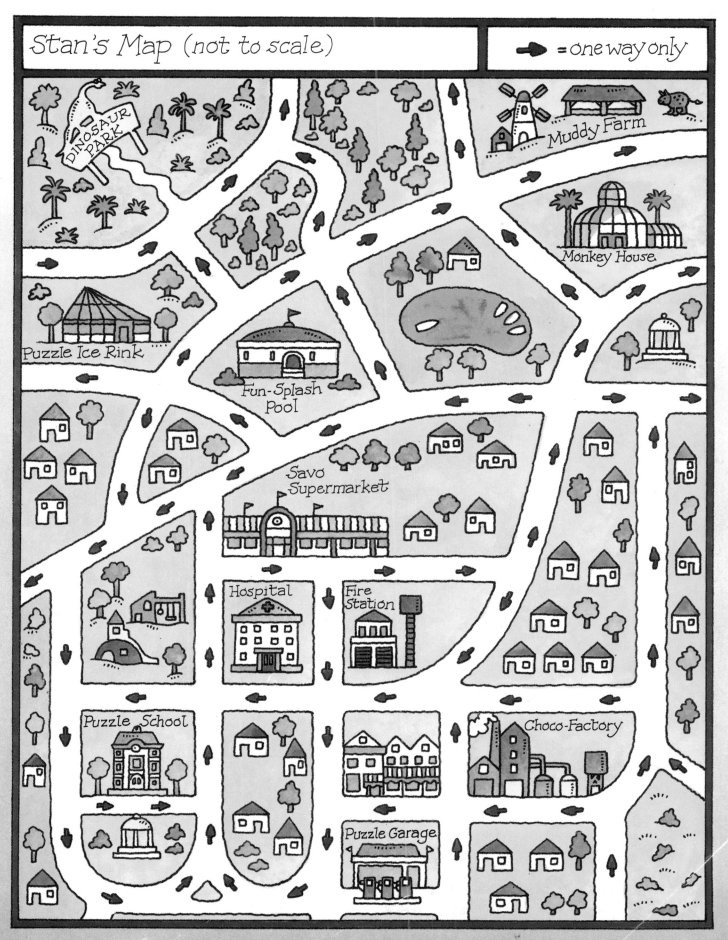

Stan's Map (not to scale)

➡ = one way only

DINOSAUR PARK

Muddy Farm

Monkey House

Puzzle Ice Rink

Fun-Splash Pool

Savo Supermarket

Hospital

Fire Station

Puzzle School

Choco-Factory

Puzzle Garage

Dinosaur park!

At last they arrived at the Dinosaur Park. It was a huge place filled with lots of model dinosaurs.

"You can look around for an hour," Miss Dibble said. "Answer these questions as you go."

She handed everyone pieces of paper. "Leave your packed lunches with me so they don't get squashed and come back at one o'clock. Have fun!"

Question 1 - Where does a diplodocus live?

Question 2 - Which dinosaur has three horns?

Question 3 - How many swings are there at the Dinosaur Park?

Question 4 - How much does a brachiosaurus weigh?

Question 5 - What is this a picture of?

Triceratops

Swamp-living Diplodocus

Brachiosaurus -very heavy

Scales

Tyrannosaurus (likes eating meat)

Greg and Jack looked at all the dinosaurs in the park, then they tried to answer the questions.

Can you find the answers to the questions?

Lunch time

At one o'clock everybody raced back to Miss Dibble. She handed out the packed lunches. But there were six lunch boxes that looked exactly the same.

"That's mine!" Greg, Jack, Katy, Amber, Ben and Ned, all shouted at once.

"Well what are you each having for lunch?" Miss Dibble asked.

They looked inside the lunch boxes and soon saw whose lunch was whose.

Do you know?

Back to school

After lunch they explored some more. Then it was time to go home.

"Everybody back on the bus," called Miss Dibble.

They lined up and Miss Dibble counted them all.

"Oh dear," she said. "There are two children missing. But who are they – and WHERE are they?"

Who is missing?

Egg

Multi-saurus

Greg knew who the missing children were. He thought he remembered seeing them hiding in the park. But where? Then he remembered.

Who is missing? Where were they?

Time to go home

At last everybody was back on the bus. Stan revved the engine and then they were off, waving goodbye to the Dinosaur Park.

When they got back to Puzzle School, there were lots of people waiting in the playground. Greg, Jack, Amber, Ben, Ned and Katy could see their parents.

Can you?

Toffee time

The next day, Mrs. Smith was back. Miss Dibble came to say goodbye.

"Thank you all for being so helpful," said Miss Dibble. "I had some tasty toffees to give you, but I think I must have dropped them yesterday. Oh dear."

"You had a hole in your pocket," said Greg. "The toffees fell out, so I picked them up. Here they are."

Everyone cheered and munched on their toffees.

Look back through the book. Can you find twelve toffees?

Model of Dinosaur Park

Answers

Pages 4-5
Getting ready

The things that Greg needs are circled here.

Pages 6-7
Walking to school

The way to Puzzle School is marked here.

Pages 8-9
In the playground

Greg's friends are circled here.

Pages 10-11
Classroom in a muddle

The changes are circled here. Greg's desk has a sun on it, like his peg.

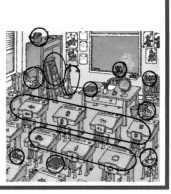

Pages 12-13
Jobs to do

It is Tuesday, so Jack is watering the plants, Amber is feeding the rabbit, Ned is sharing the pencils, Katy is handing out the writing books and Greg is wiping the blackboard. The things that they need are circled here.

Pages 14-15
Miss Dibble is confused

The rabbit should go in the rabbit hutch. The song sheets should go in the music box. The paints should go in the art cupboard. The pencils should go in the pencil pot. The books should go on the book shelf and Amber's photo should go in her satchel.

Pages 16-17
In the hall

The class circled in red is going skating. The class circled in green is going to Muddy Farm. The class circled in blue is going swimming. Mr. Brain's class is going to the Choco Factory. So Greg's class must be going to the Dinosaur Park.

Pages 18-19
Bus trouble

Katy has spotted that the oil tank is empty!

Pages 20-21
Map reading

Their route from Puzzle School to the Dinosaur Park is marked in red. They are here.

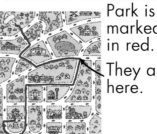

Pages 22-23
Dinosaur park!

1 – A Diplodocus lives in a swamp.

2 – A Triceratops has three horns.

3 – There are five swings and a swing boat.

4 – A Brachiosaurus weighs 80 tons!

5 – It is the foot of a Tyrannosaurus.

Pages 24-25
Lunch time

a = Greg's lunch.
b = Jack's lunch.
c = Amber's lunch.
d = Ben's lunch.
e = Ned's lunch.
f = Katy's lunch.

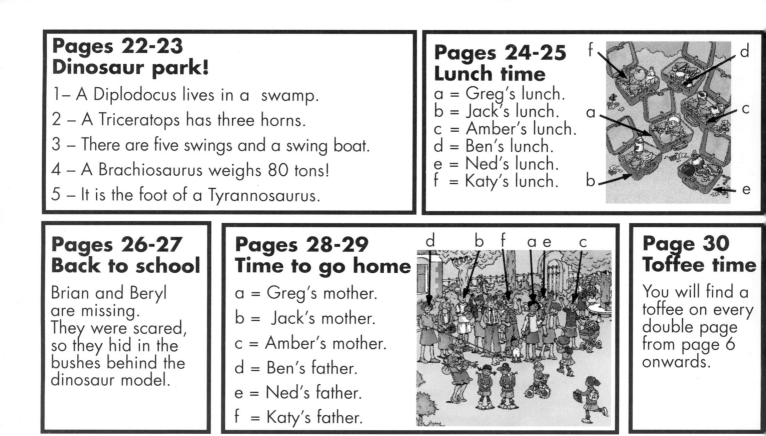

Pages 26-27
Back to school

Brian and Beryl are missing. They were scared, so they hid in the bushes behind the dinosaur model.

Pages 28-29
Time to go home

a = Greg's mother.
b = Jack's mother.
c = Amber's mother.
d = Ben's father.
e = Ned's father.
f = Katy's father.

Page 30
Toffee time

You will find a toffee on every double page from page 6 onwards.

Did you spot everything?
Puzzle School pencils

Miss Dibble's things

Beryl and Brian

The chart below shows you how many Puzzle School pencils are hiding on each double page. You can also find out where Miss Dibble has lost her things.

Did you remember to watch out for the mischievous Beryl and Brian? Look back through the book again and see if you can spot them.

Pages	Puzzle School pencils	Miss Dibble's things
6-7	two	scary things book
8-9	three	paint box
10-11	four	pencil
12-13	four	recorder
14-15	three	chalk
16-17	five	cup of tea
18-19	two	glue
20-21	two	key
22-23	four	tissues
24-25	two	scissors
26-27	three	glasses
28-29	none	whistle

First published in 1996 by Usborne Publishing Ltd, Usborne House, 83-85 Saffron Hill, London EC1N 8RT, England.

Copyright © 1996 Usborne Publishing Ltd.

The name Usborne and the device ⊕ are Trade Marks of Usborne Publishing Ltd. All rights reserved. No part of this publication may be reproduced, stored in a retrieval system, or transmitted in any form or by any means, electronic, mechanical, photocopying, recording or otherwise, without the prior permission of the publisher.

Printed in Portugal

First published in America March 1997   UE